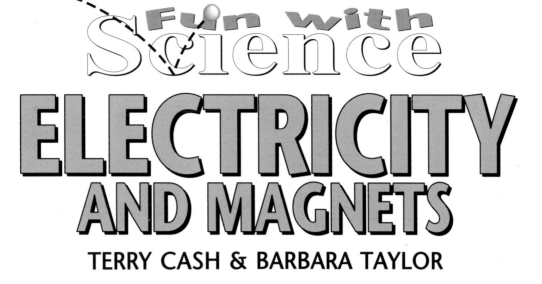

Fun with Science
ELECTRICITY
AND MAGNETS

TERRY CASH & BARBARA TAYLOR

Contents

Use the symbols below to help you
identify the three kinds of practical
activities in this book.

EXPERIMENTS   TRICKS   THINGS TO MAKE

Kingfisher

Introduction

Without electricity, life as we know it would come to an end. There would be no easy way to make light or heat, to cook our food or keep clean. Think of all the machines in your home or school which need batteries or have to be plugged into an electrical socket to make them work. Yet less than 100 years ago, electricity was a strange, new invention.

The first part of this book will tell you how electricity was first discovered and how it is generated in batteries and power stations. There are plenty of ideas for safe experiments using batteries and bulbs to make circuits and switches. In the second half of the book, you can investigate the mysterious force called magnetism and find out more about the links between electricity and magnetism.

The questions on the opposite page are based on the ideas explained in this book. As you carry out the experiments, you will be able to answer these questions and come to understand the importance of electricity in our world.

This book covers seven main topics:
- Static electricity; lightning
- Current electricity; power stations; batteries
- Circuits and switches; conductors and insulators
- Magnetic forces
- Magnetic poles; compasses
- Electro-magnets
- Animals and electricity; electrical machines

A blue line (like the one around the edge of these two pages) indicates the start of a new topic.

Equipment you will need

All the experiments in this book use batteries. These are safe to use for experiments with electricity. Here are some of the things you will need:

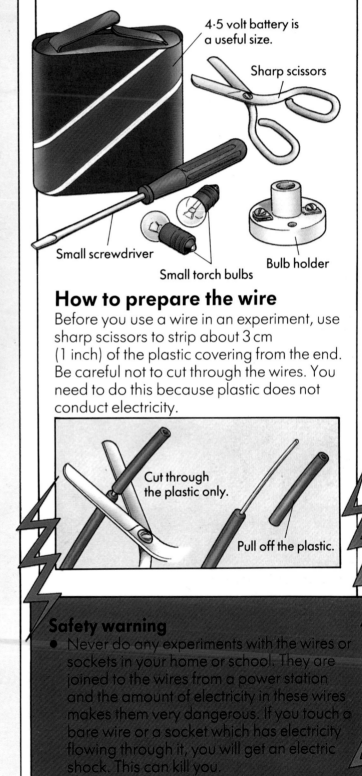

4·5 volt battery is a useful size.

Sharp scissors

Small screwdriver

Small torch bulbs

Bulb holder

How to prepare the wire

Before you use a wire in an experiment, use sharp scissors to strip about 3 cm (1 inch) of the plastic covering from the end. Be careful not to cut through the wires. You need to do this because plastic does not conduct electricity.

Cut through the plastic only.

Pull off the plastic.

Safety warning
- Never do any experiments with the wires or sockets in your home or school. They are joined to the wires from a power station and the amount of electricity in these wires makes them very dangerous. If you touch a bare wire or a socket which has electricity flowing through it, you will get an electric shock. This can kill you.

- Do not go near electricity pylons, overhead cables or substations. High voltage electricity can jump across a gap and kill you.

◄ How can you make a burglar alarm using a pressure switch? (page 17)

► If one Christmas tree light bulb goes, why do all the other lights go out? (page 15)

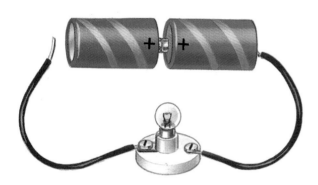

► How can you get electricity from a lemon? (page 13)

▲ Will this bulb light up if you complete the circuit? (page 14)

▼ Without any glue, how can you make pieces of paper stick to a comb? (page 4)

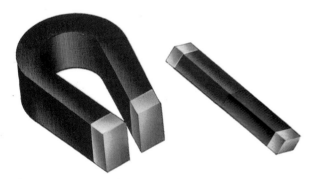

▲ Are horseshoe magnets stronger than bar magnets? (page 25)

▼ Why does lightning often strike tall buildings? (page 8)

▼ How can you make an electro-magnetic crane? (pages 34 and 35)

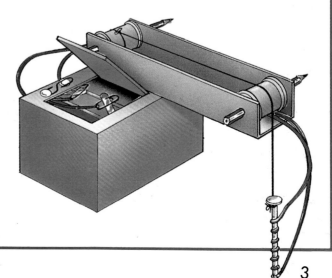

Static Electricity

Electricity was first discovered by the Greeks in about 600 B C A man called Thales found that when he rubbed a piece of amber with some cloth, the amber attracted small objects. (Amber is hardened sap from trees.)

In about A D 1570 an Englishman called William Gilbert carried out similar investigations. He called the effects he saw '**electricity**,' after the Greek word for amber, which is *elektron*. The type of electricity with which Thales and Gilbert experimented is called **static electricity**, which means it does not move.

Hint
All experiments and tricks with static electricity work best on cold, dry days. Plastic and nylon hold static electricity better than other substances.

Making Static

You can make static electricity by rubbing things together.

Equipment: A plastic comb, a woollen jumper, tiny scraps of tissue paper.
Rub the comb several times on the woollen jumper. Then hold the comb close to the pieces of tissue paper. What happens to the paper?

How it works
When the comb is rubbed on the jumper, it becomes charged with static electricity and attracts the pieces of paper.

Static charges can be positive or negative. An object with one kind of static charge will attract an object with the opposite charge. In this experiment, the comb has a negative charge and it attracts the paper, which has a positive charge.

Bending Water Trick

Rub a plastic comb to charge it with static electricity and then turn on a tap so the water runs in a thin stream. Hold your charged comb close to the water and watch what happens to the water.

How it works
The water will bend towards the comb because it is attracted by the static electricity in the comb.

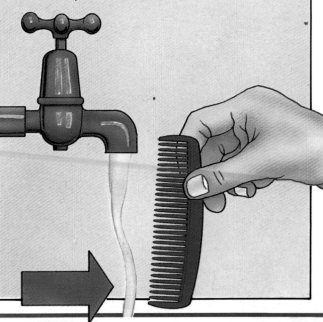

Sticky Balloons

This trick shows you how to stick a balloon to the wall without using any glue.

Rub a balloon several times on a woollen jumper and then hold it against a wall. The strong static charge on the plastic skin of the balloon will make it cling to the wall as if it is glued there.

How it works

There is a difference between the charge on the balloon and the charge on the wall, so the balloon is pulled towards the wall. It will stay there until the static charge wears off. How long did your balloon stay on the wall?

The Unfriendly Balloons

If you bring together two objects which have the same kind of static charge, strange things can happen. Ask a friend to help you with this experiment.

1. Tie two balloons together with a piece of thread.

2. Ask your friend to hold a thin stick straight out in front of them. Hang the thread over the stick so the balloons are next to each other.

3. Then rub each balloon long and hard with a woollen jumper.

4. When you let the balloons go, they will try to push each other away.

How it works

When you rub the balloons, you are giving them the same kind of static charge. Things that have the same charge try to push away (**repel**) each other.

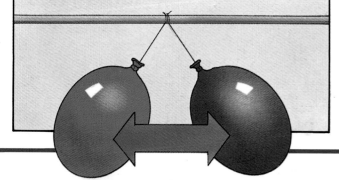

▲ Static electricity can make your hair stand on end! This girl is touching a Van der Graaff generator which gives out a positive charge, making all the hairs on the girl's head have the same static charge. Each hair tries to push away from the next one (because things with the same charge repel), so the girl's hair stands on end.

Rolling Tricks

Rub the plastic pen very hard with the felt or wool. Put the table tennis ball on a smooth table top and hold the pen close to the ball. The ball will seem to move at the command of your 'magic wand'. Which way does it roll, towards your wand or away from it?

Equipment: A plastic pen, felt or woollen material, a table tennis ball, plastic drinking straws.

Now put three plastic straws on the table and arrange them to match the picture. Rub the pen with the felt or wool and hold the side of the pen close to the straw which is on top of others. Can you work out why some things move towards the pen and others move away?

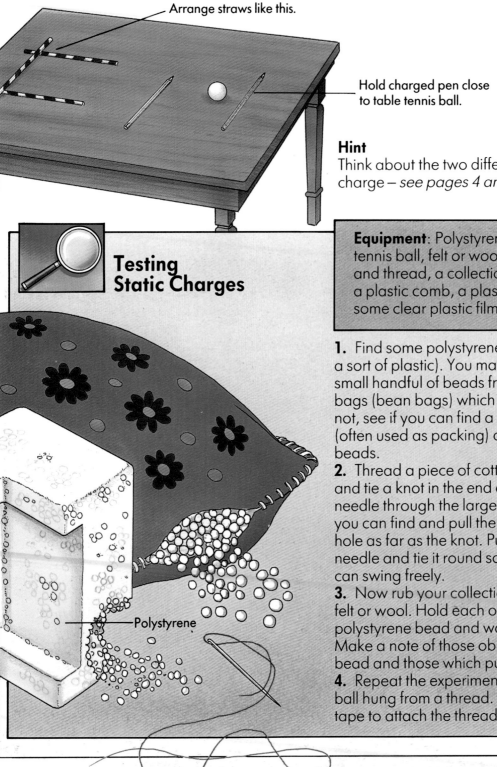

Arrange straws like this.

Hold charged pen close to table tennis ball.

Hint
Think about the two different kinds of static charge – *see pages 4 and 5*.

Testing Static Charges

Polystyrene

Equipment: Polystyrene beads, a table tennis ball, felt or woollen material, needle and thread, a collection of objects such as a plastic comb, a plastic pen, a balloon, some clear plastic film, a plastic bag.

1. Find some polystyrene beads (polystyrene is a sort of plastic). You may be able to get a small handful of beads from one of those saggy bags (bean bags) which are used as seats. If not, see if you can find a block of polystyrene (often used as packing) and break off some beads.

2. Thread a piece of cotton through the needle and tie a knot in the end of the thread. Push the needle through the largest polystyrene bead you can find and pull the thread through the hole as far as the knot. Pull the cotton out of the needle and tie it round something so the bead can swing freely.

3. Now rub your collection of objects with the felt or wool. Hold each one in turn close to the polystyrene bead and watch what happens. Make a note of those objects which attract the bead and those which push it away.

4. Repeat the experiment with a table tennis ball hung from a thread. (Use a small piece of tape to attach the thread to the ball.)

Separate Salt from Pepper

Equipment: Salt, pepper (finely ground), a plastic comb or pen, felt or wool.

Sprinkle a little salt and pepper on to a plate. Rub the pen or comb very hard with the felt or wool. Hold the pen or comb very close to the plate and move it slowly over the salt and pepper mixture. The pepper will jump up to the pen or comb but the salt will stay behind.

How it works
Both the salt and the pepper are attracted by the static charges on the pen or comb, but the pepper rises first because it is lighter than the salt. If you hold the pen or comb too close to the plate, you will pick up the salt as well.

Are the movements the same for the polystyrene bead and the table tennis ball? What can you discover about the static charges on the objects you have rubbed?

Hint
Try and work out which objects must have the same charge as the bead or ball and which objects must have different charges. If you get stuck, look back at pages 4 and 5.

Sticky tape

Table tennis ball

Thread

Polystyrene bead

Electricity in the Sky

Although you may not realize it, you will already have come across one kind of static electricity. This is the powerful 'electricity in the sky' which we call **lightning**.

Crackles and Sparks

Have you ever seen little flashes and sparks of light when you undress in the dark? These sparks are the static electricity which is made by your clothes rubbing together.

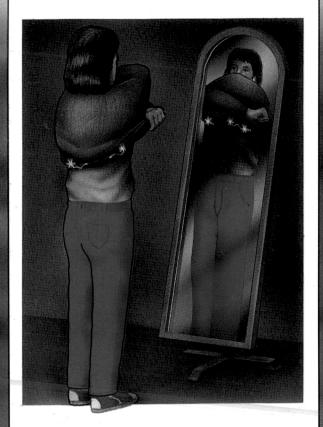

Wear a nylon shirt under a woollen jumper and stand in front of a mirror in a dark room. When you pull off the jumper, you should see the sparks fly.

During a storm, you can see giant sparks of static electricity when lightning flashes across the sky.

Electricity in Clouds

In a storm cloud, the moving air makes tiny water droplets and ice particles rub together so they become charged with static electricity. The positively-charged particles rise to the top of the cloud and the negatively-charged particles sink to the bottom of the cloud.

The negative charges in the cloud are strongly attracted to the ground. They leap from cloud to cloud or from the cloud to the ground as giant flashes of lightning. The lightning makes the air so hot that it explodes with loud booms of thunder.

In 1753, an American scientist, Benjamin Franklin, decided to investigate the charge in storm clouds. He did this in an experiment that was so dangerous he was lucky not to have been killed. **Never even think** of trying the same experiment yourself.

On a stormy day he flew a large kite on a very long line up into a black, mountainous storm cloud. He tied a large iron key to the bottom of his line and when the electrical charge ran down the wet kite line and hit the key, sparks flashed. Luckily he was not hurt and his investigations led to the invention of lightning conductors.

Lightning often strikes the first point it reaches on its journey to the ground, so tall buildings are most likely to be hit. If you look up at church spires and tall buildings, you can sometimes see a metal strip going down the side of the building. This is called a **lightning conductor** and it is usually made of copper.

If lightning strikes the top of the building, electricity will flow safely down the copper strip to the earth instead of damaging the building.

How far is the Storm?

Light travels so quickly (about 300,000 kilometres – 186,416 miles – in one **second**!) that we see a bright flash of lightning instantly. But we have to wait a few moments before we hear the thunder. This is because sound travels much more slowly than light – at only 330 metres in one second (750 miles in an hour).

During a storm, wait until you see a flash of lightning, then start to count slowly. For every count of three, the storm is roughly one kilometre away (a count of five means the storm is about one mile away).

Warning
If you are caught in a thunderstorm do **not** shelter under a tree, especially one that is tall or standing on its own. The lightning may strike the tree and hit you as well.

Electricity on the Move

The electricity we use in our homes and schools is different from static electricity because it moves from place to place. It flows through wires in the same way that water flows through a hose. We call this flow an electric **current**.

Spot the Difference

Can you spot the differences between these two pictures?

In the bottom picture, there are no electric gadgets. Nowadays, we use electricity for so many things it's hard to imagine life without it.

Making Electricity

An electric current was first generated in 1831 by Michael Faraday. He moved a magnet in and out of a coil of wire and found that this made an electric current flow through the wire.

This was a very important discovery which led to the invention of the **dynamo**. Nowadays, we still use dynamos to make almost all our electricity and much of our present way of life is based on Faraday's discovery.

Testing a Dynamo

On some bicycles, the lights are powered by a simple dynamo. The movement of the wheels makes a magnet turn round inside a coil of wire. This makes electricity flow in the wire and the lights come on.

If you or your friends have a bicycle with a dynamo, try this test. Turn the bicycle upside down and balance it on the handle bars and the saddle. Switch on the front light and turn the pedals slowly at first, then quickly. What happens to the light as the dynamo is turned faster? Why might this be dangerous if you are cycling at night?

Drive wheel

Coil of wire

Magnet

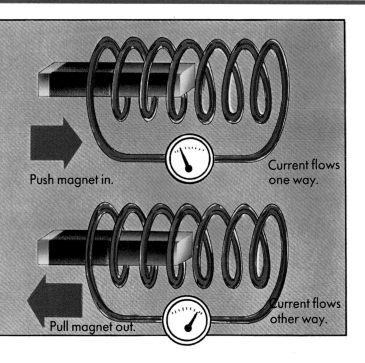

Push magnet in. — Current flows one way.

Pull magnet out. — Current flows other way.

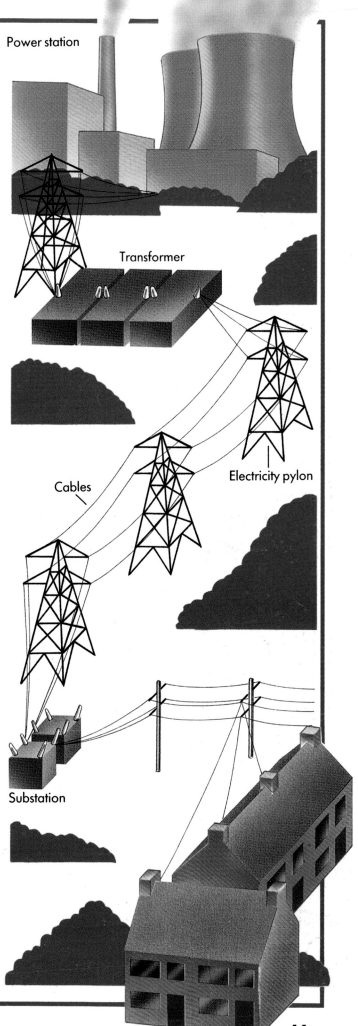

Power station

Transformer

Electricity pylon

Cables

Substation

Power Stations

Most of the electricity we use in our homes, schools, shops and factories is made (**generated**) in power stations. In a power station, fuel such as coal or oil is burned to heat water and turn it into steam. The steam pushes a huge wheel, called a **turbine**, round at very high speeds. The turbine turns a massive dynamo called a **generator**, which makes electricity.

From the power station, the electricity is carried along thick wires called **cables** until it reaches our homes or other buildings. The wires may be buried under the ground or they may be hung from tall towers called **pylons**.

To send the electricity over long distances, it first goes through a device called a **transformer**. This increases the voltage of the electricity, (voltage is the pressure which pushes electricity along a wire) and makes it cheaper to move. When the electricity reaches towns or cities, the power is reduced back to the right level for the machines we use by another transformer.

Warning
The electricity in your home is very dangerous; it can easily kill you. **Never** play with plugs, sockets, wires or anything connected to the mains supply.

11

Battery Power

Even though you must never do experiments with mains electricity, you can discover a lot about electricity in complete safety using small batteries and bulbs. Batteries are useful because they are small enough to be carried from place to place.

▲ Alessandro Volta (*right*) demonstrates his Voltaic pile to Napoleon.

The First Battery

The first battery was made in 1800 by an Italian scientist, Alessandro Volta. Volta discovered that some metals and a liquid could work together to produce electricity.

He made a 'sandwich' of paper soaked in salt water between a piece of silver and a piece of zinc. When he joined the two metals with a wire, he found that a current flowed through the wire. As the current was very weak, he made a pile of his 'sandwiches' and when he touched a wire from the top of the pile to a wire from the bottom, he got sparks of electricity. Volta's battery came to be known as the **Voltaic pile**.

Did you know that the electrical measurement the '**volt**' was named after Volta? The number of volts describes the pressure or '**voltage**' which pushes electricity along a wire.

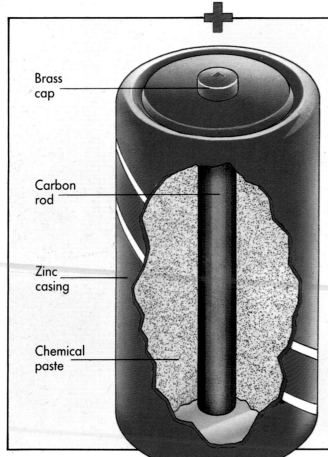

Brass cap

Carbon rod

Zinc casing

Chemical paste

How a Battery Works

The batteries we use today work in a similar way to the battery made by Volta. The case of a battery is made of zinc metal; this is often covered with card and plastic or tin to prevent the battery from leaking. Instead of a piece of silver or copper, there is a carbon rod (rather like a thick pencil lead) in the middle of the battery. The battery case is not filled with salt water because this would easily leak out. Instead, there is a chemical paste between the carbon and the zinc casing.

The chemicals in the battery make electricity. As the electricity is taken from the battery, the chemicals are slowly used up. Eventually, the battery cannot make electricity any more. Some batteries, such as those used in cars, can be recharged so they go on working for longer.

Make your own Battery

Equipment: Two pieces of wire about 15 cm (6 inches) long, 4 shiny copper coins, tin foil, blotting paper, salty water.

1. Cut the foil and blotting paper into small squares the same size as the coins.

2. Pour plenty of salt into a beaker of water and leave the blotting paper to soak for a while.

3. Carefully place a square of foil on top of one coin, with a piece of salty blotting paper on top of the foil.

4. Repeat these three layers in the same order until you have made a small pile.

5. Place the end of one wire underneath the pile and the end of the other wire on the top of the pile.

6. Now touch both the free ends of the wires lightly on your tongue. Can you feel a tingle of electricity?

How it works

In your voltaic pile, chemical reactions cause a tiny electric current. The current flows from one wire, through your tongue and into the other wire. The current is just enough to make your tongue tingle.

Wire

Salty blotting paper

Foil

Coin

Can you get Electricity from a Lemon?

First press the lemon gently on a table to make it juicy inside. Then stick a strip of zinc and a strip of copper (or copper and zinc nails) into the lemon. Make sure that the two metals are not touching. If you touch the two pieces of metal with your tongue, you should be able to feel a tingle of electricity.

This is because the metal strips react with the acid in the lemon juice to make electricity. A tiny electric current passes through your tongue.

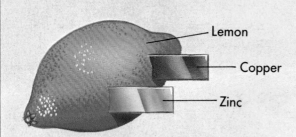

Lemon

Copper

Zinc

▶ At the Launch Pad in the Science Museum, London, the child's slightly damp and salty hands link the two metal plates together and a current flows from one to the other.

Investigating Circuits

To make electricity come out of a battery, you need to give it a path, such as a wire, to move along. Electricity can only move in one direction, so you need to attach a wire from one end (**terminal**) of the battery to the other end. This loop of wire is called a **circuit**. As long as the circuit is complete, electricity will flow. If there is a gap in the circuit, electricity will not be able to flow. It's rather like a toy train on its track. If there are any gaps, the train will not run around the circuit.

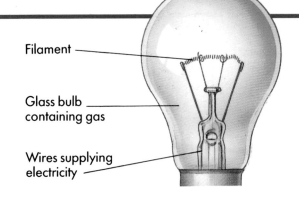

Filament

Glass bulb containing gas

Wires supplying electricity

▲ Electricity flows into a light bulb and out again. The wire filament is so thin that the electricity has to push hard to get through the wire. This makes the filament white hot so that it glows with a bright light. The filament is made of a metal called tungsten which can get very hot before it melts. The glass bulb is filled with a gas which helps to stop the filament from burning away too quickly.

Make a Simple Circuit

All you need is a battery, some wire and a small torch bulb.

See if you can make the bulb light up. Look carefully at the bulb. Can you see where you need to touch the wires? Don't forget that electricity can only flow if a circuit is complete.

How it works
To make the bulb light up, electricity must flow out of one end of the battery, through the bulb and back to the other end of the battery.
Inside the bulb, can you see a tiny coiled

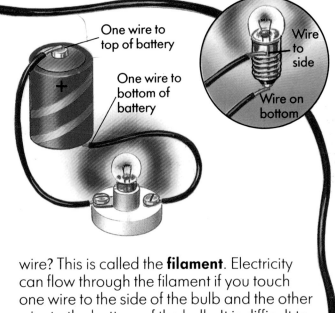

One wire to top of battery

One wire to bottom of battery

Wire to side

Wire on bottom

wire? This is called the **filament**. Electricity can flow through the filament if you touch one wire to the side of the bulb and the other wire to the bottom of the bulb. It is difficult to hold the wires and the bulb together but you can use a bulb holder to do the job for you.

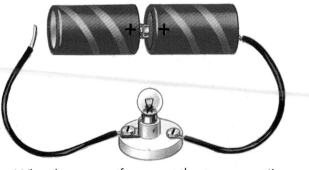

What happens if you link two batteries into your circuit?

What happens if you put the two negative or the two positive battery ends together?

Glowing Wool Trick

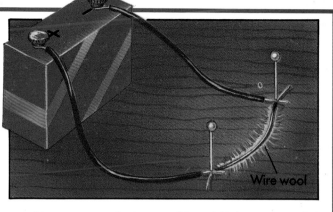

Equipment: A battery, two wires, some steel wool (the kind used for cleaning metal pots and pans).

Pull out one long strand of steel wool and pin it to a board. Attach one wire to one end of the battery and the other wire to the other end. With the free ends of both wires, touch the strand of steel wool. What happens?

How it works
The electrical current flows easily through the wires but has more difficulty passing through the thin strand of steel wool. This makes the

Wire wool

steel heat up and glow red hot. With a powerful battery, it may even melt and break.

There are very thin wires in the **fuses** which are fitted into the electrical machines, circuits and plugs in our homes. If something goes wrong with the wiring, the thin fuse wire quickly melts and makes a gap in the circuit. This cuts off the electricity supply and prevents a fire.

Circuit Challenge

Can you link three bulbs to one battery so that all three bulbs light up at the same time? When you have done this, try taking one of the bulbs out of the circuit. Do the other bulbs go out as well?

How it works
There are two different ways of wiring several bulbs into a circuit. One way is to

wire up all the bulbs on one circuit. This is called a **series** circuit. The bulbs give out only a dim light because they are all sharing the same power. If you take out one bulb, it breaks the circuit and the other bulbs go out as well.

The other way of wiring up the bulbs is to give each bulb a separate circuit. These are called **parallel** circuits. If you wire up your three bulbs like this, each bulb will look almost as bright as one bulb in a circuit on its own. If you take out one bulb, the other bulbs will all stay on.

▼ Christmas tree lights are wired up in a series circuit. If one bulb goes, all the lights go out.

Series circuit

Parallel circuit

Experiment with Conductors and Insulators

Some materials let electricity flow through them. They are called **conductors**. Other materials stop electricity passing through them. They are called **insulators**. We use conductors to carry electricity to where it is needed and we use insulators to stop it leaking into places where we do not want it to be.

Try this experiment to find out which materials are conductors and which are insulators.

To hold a wire on to a battery terminal, hook it around a paper clip.

▲ Cables from a power station carry electricity at a very high voltage. Ceramic insulators are used to stop the dangerous current from leaking out and causing damage or injuries. These insulators are in a sub-station, but you can also see them on electricity pylons.

Equipment: Battery, bulb and bulb holder, some wires, a collection of objects to test. Choose things such as a coin, a paper clip, a plastic pen top, a glass bottle, a fork, a wooden spoon, tin foil, cardboard, a key, an eraser, a stone.

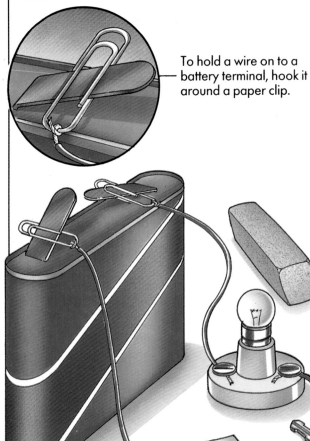

1. Make a circuit like the one in the picture.
2. Touch the wires together to make sure the bulb lights up and there are no loose connections.
3. Now touch the ends of both wires to the objects in your collection. Does the bulb light up?

4. Put all the things which made the bulb light up into one pile. These are the conductors. They conduct electricity through themselves and complete the circuit. What are they made from?
5. Put all the things that did not make the bulb light up into another pile. They are insulators. What are the insulators made from?

Bridging the Gap

Equipment: A battery, a bulb and bulb holder, some wires, two metal drawing pins, a metal paper clip, a piece of wood about 8 cm by 5 cm (3 by 2 inches).

A **switch** is a gap in a circuit that can be bridged easily. When a switch is pressed 'on', the gap is closed and the circuit is complete. The electric current can then flow to make a bulb light up or a machine work.

Try making your own switch.
1. Push the drawing pins into the piece of wood. Keep them a little way apart.
2. Trap one wire under one drawing pin and the other wire under the other drawing pin. Join the other ends of the wires to the battery and bulb.
3. Open up the paper clip and hook one end under one drawing pin.
4. To 'switch on', touch the paper clip on to the other drawing pin to complete the circuit.
5. You can 'switch off' the bulb by moving the paper clip away from the drawing pin.

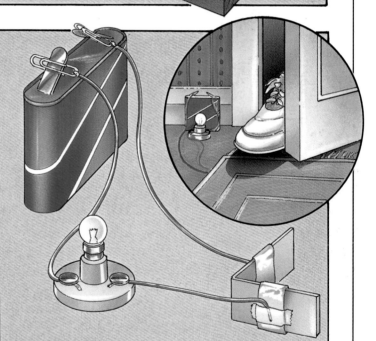

Paper clip switch

Drawing pin

Make a Burglar Alarm

Equipment: A battery, some wires, thin card, tin foil, sticky tape or glue, a small buzzer (from an electrical shop). If you can't get a buzzer, use a bulb in a bulb holder instead.

1. Cut a piece of card about 15 cm by 7.5 cm (6 by 3 inches) and fold it in half.
2. Tape strips of tin foil around the card.

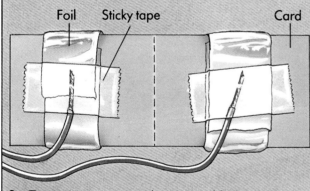

Foil   Sticky tape   Card

3. Tape a wire to each piece of foil.
4. Join the wires into a circuit with the battery and the buzzer or bulb.

5. Set up your burglar alarm near a door so that anyone coming through the door will tread on the card and set off the buzzer or make the bulb light up.

How it works
When the two pieces of foil are pressed together, the circuit is complete and electricity can flow.

Turn on the Light

Try adding lights and switches to a doll's house so you can turn on a light upstairs or downstairs.

Equipment: Large cardboard box, sheets of thin card, paste, glue or sticky tape, 2 bulbs, 2 bulb holders, wire, battery, 4 brass paper fasteners, 2 metal paper clips, doll's house furniture, old pieces of wallpaper and carpet.

1. Make your doll's house from a cardboard box turned on its side. To make a ceiling and some stairs, glue or tape sheets of thin card inside the box.

2. Put the bulbs into the bulb holders and fix two long wires to each holder.

3. Cut a small hole in the ceiling of each room and push the bulbs through the holes.

4. Push the paper fasteners through the side of the box and use the paper clips to make two switches.

5. Connect up the wires to the bulbs, the switches and the battery to make two parallel circuits with a switch on each loop (*see diagram*).

6. Add some decorations and furniture.

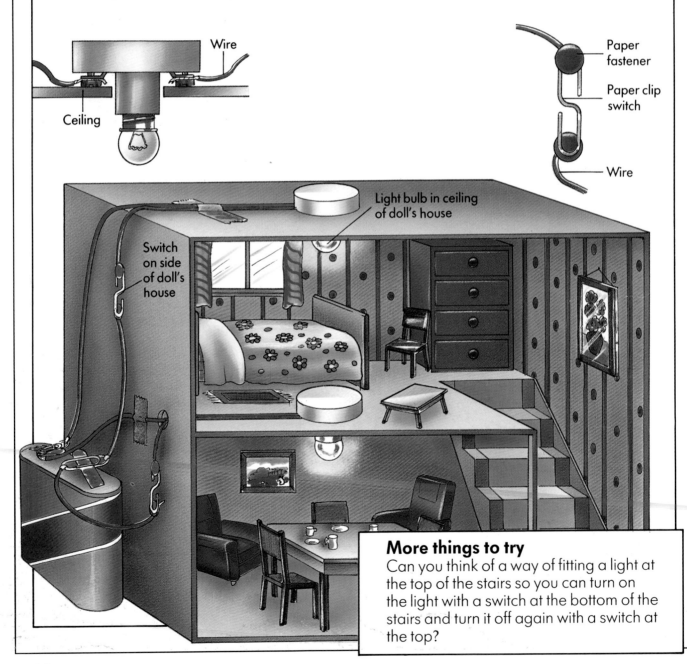

Wire

Ceiling

Paper fastener

Paper clip switch

Wire

Switch on side of doll's house

Light bulb in ceiling of doll's house

More things to try

Can you think of a way of fitting a light at the top of the stairs so you can turn on the light with a switch at the bottom of the stairs and turn it off again with a switch at the top?

Make a Lighthouse

Equipment: An empty washing-up liquid bottle, bulb, bulb holder, battery, wire, scissors, tape, glue, newspaper, paper clip switch, stiff card or wooden board about 20 cm (8 inches) square, thin card, plaster of paris or papier mâché, a clear plastic or glass pot.

1. Pull off the top of the bottle and use the scissors to cut off the bottom of the bottle.
2. Cut two pieces of wire which are both about 15 cm (6 inches) longer than the bottle and join one wire to either side of the bulb holder.
3. Put the bulb into the holder and push the holder up inside the bottle so the bulb comes out of the hole at the top.
4. Tape or glue the bulb holder in place. If you find this difficult, screw up some newspaper and put this inside the bottle to wedge the bulb in place.
5. Glue or tape the plastic or glass pot to the top of the bottle.
6. Make a box out of the thin card and put it (upside down) over the battery.
7. Push some paper fasteners through the top of the box and attach a paper clip to one of the fasteners to make a switch.
8. Join one of the wires from the bulb holder to the switch and the other wire to one of the battery terminals. Join the switch to the other battery terminal with a new piece of wire.
9. Stand the bottle and the box on the thick card or wood.
10. Make up the plaster of paris or the papier mâché and mould it around the bottom of the bottle to make some rocks. Leave a gap around the box so you can lift it up to change the battery.
11. Paint the rocks and the lighthouse.

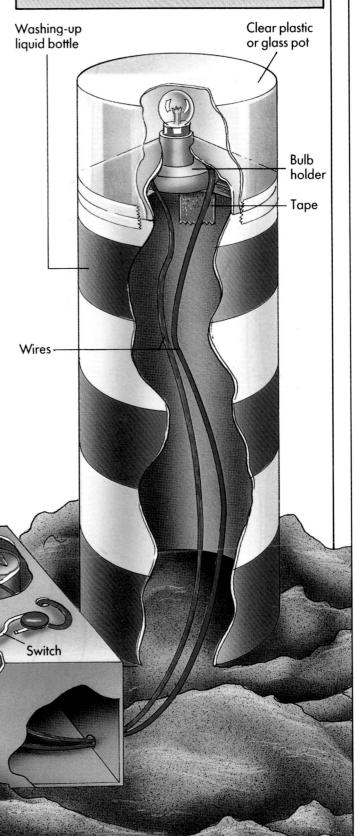

Washing-up liquid bottle

Clear plastic or glass pot

Bulb holder

Tape

Wires

Battery

Cardboard box

Plaster or papier mâché 'rocks'

Switch

Steady Hand Game

Equipment: A block of wood about 50 cm by 20 cm (16 inches by 8 inches), a wire coat hanger, pair of strong pliers, a hammer, wire staples (from a hardware store), battery, bulb in a bulb holder, wire, sticky tape.

Ask an adult to help you make this game.

1. Use the pliers to cut a short piece of wire from the coat hanger. Bend the wire into a loop but leave the end open.

2. Join a short length of wire to the open loop and join the other end of this wire to the bulb holder.

3. With another piece of wire, join the other side of the bulb holder to the battery.

4. Bend the rest of the coat hanger into a long, wavy line.

5. Wind tape round both ends of this wavy line of wire. (When you are not playing the game, you can rest the loop against this tape and the bulb will not light up.)

6. Join one end of the wavy wire to the battery with some wire.

7. Put the wavy wire on to the wooden board and hammer a wire staple over each end of the wire to hold it upright.

8. Bend the end of the open loop around the wavy wire and join up the loop with the pliers.

9. Decorate the board with paints or crayons.

10. Try replacing the bulb with a small buzzer.

How to play the game

Can you or your friends move the loop all the way along the wavy line without making the bulb flash? If your hand shakes, the loop will touch the wire and complete the circuit. Electricity will flow along the wire and the bulb will flash.

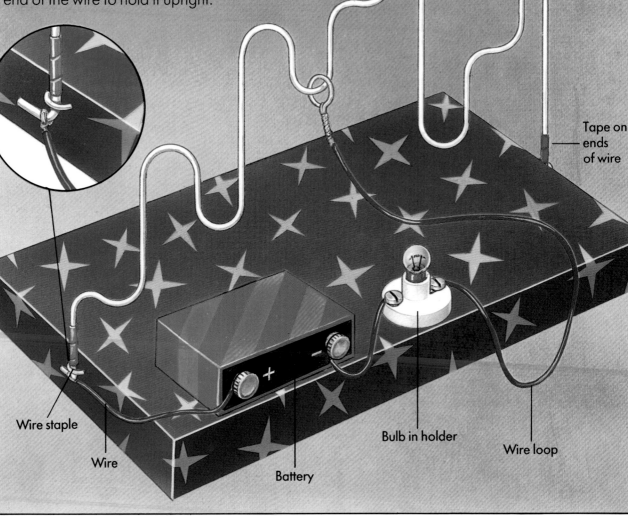

Tape on ends of wire

Wire staple

Wire

Battery

Bulb in holder

Wire loop

Electronic Quiz Game

Make a quiz game with a light that flashes to show the right answer.

1. On one side of the card, glue or tape some pieces of paper with the questions on the left and the answers on the right. Muddle them up so each question is next to the wrong answer.

2. Push a paper fastener through the card next to each question and each answer.

3. Turn the quiz board over and join up each question to the right answer with a piece of wire. Loop the wire around the back of the paper fasteners.

4. With some more wire, join the battery to the bulb holder as shown in the diagram.

5. Join some more wire to the other side of the battery and the other side of the bulb holder. Leave the ends of both these wires free.

Equipment: A piece of stiff card about 30 cm (1 foot) square, paper, pen, scissors, pins, brass paper fasteners, wire, battery, bulb in a bulb holder, sticky tape, glue.

How to play the game

Ask a friend to hold one of the loose wires on a paper fastener next to a question and the other loose wire on a paper fastener next to the answer they think is the right one. If they are correct, they will complete a circuit and the bulb will light up.

More things to try

Make up some different questions and answers for your quiz board but don't forget to connect each question to the correct answer on the back of the board.

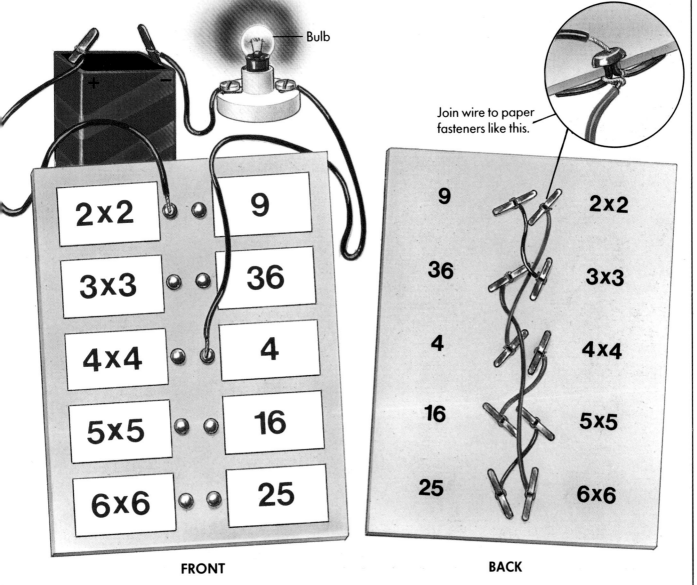

Bulb

Join wire to paper fasteners like this.

FRONT

2x2   9
3x3   36
4x4   4
5x5   16
6x6   25

BACK

9   2x2
36   3x3
4   4x4
16   5x5
25   6x6

Make a Morse Code Transmitter

In 1838, an American, Samuel Morse, invented a way of sending messages by means of electrical signals. He worked out a code of short and long sounds or flashes of light which represented all the letters of the alphabet. The code was named the **Morse Code** after its inventor.

You can send messages from one room to another by making a simple morse code transmitter.

Equipment: Two wires long enough to stretch between the two rooms, two bulbs in bulb holders (or two small buzzers), two batteries, two paper clip switches (*see page 17*).

1. Make two switches but bend the paper clips up in the air above the drawing pins.
2. Connect the batteries and bulbs at the ends of the two long wires to match the diagram.
3. When you touch the drawing pin with the paper clip, you will complete the circuit and both bulbs and buzzers will work. This means you can see the messages you are sending as well as the ones you receive.
4. To send your messages, use the morse code or make up your own secret code.

▲ An operator sends a message on a Morse-printing telegraph.

Morse Code

a	● ━		s	● ● ●
b	━ ● ● ●		t	━
c	━ ● ━ ●		u	● ● ━
d	━ ● ●		v	● ● ● ━
e	●		w	● ━ ━
f	● ● ━ ●		x	━ ● ● ━
g	━ ━ ●		y	━ ● ━ ━
h	● ● ● ●		z	━ ━ ● ●
i	● ●		1	● ━ ━ ━ ━
j	● ━ ━ ━		2	● ● ━ ━ ━
k	━ ● ━		3	● ● ● ━ ━
l	● ━ ● ●		4	● ● ● ● ━
m	━ ━		5	● ● ● ● ●
n	━ ●		6	━ ● ● ● ●
o	━ ━ ━		7	━ ━ ● ● ●
p	● ━ ━ ●		8	━ ━ ━ ● ●
q	━ ━ ● ━		9	━ ━ ━ ━ ●
r	● ━ ●		0	━ ━ ━ ━ ━

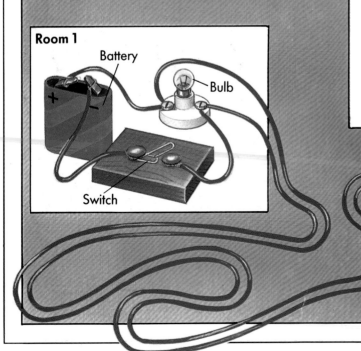

Room 1
Battery
Bulb
Switch

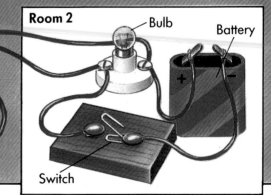

Room 2
Bulb
Battery
Switch

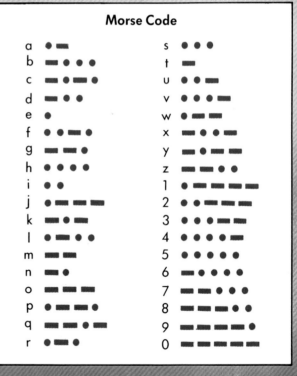

Make your own Torch

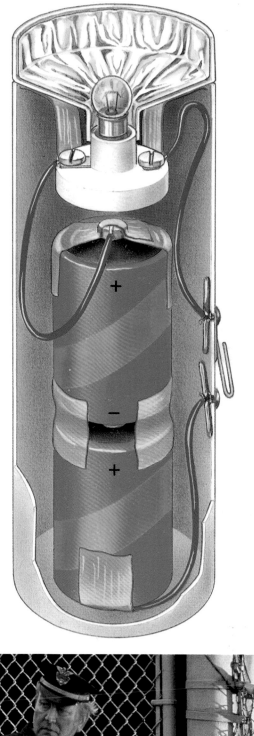

Sometimes it is very useful to be able to carry an electric light about with you. With a torch, you can see in the dark anywhere and at any time.

Here's how to make your own torch.

Equipment: An empty washing-up liquid bottle, scissors, tin foil, glue, sticky tape, bulb in a bulb holder, 2 brass paper fasteners, paper clip, wire, 2 batteries.

1. Pull off the cap from the washing-up bottle.
2. Use the scissors to cut off the top of the bottle. Turn it upside down to make a funnel.
3. On the inside of the funnel, glue some tin foil.
4. Push the bulb in its holder up inside the neck of the funnel and hold it in position with tape or glue.
5. To make a switch, push the two paper fasteners through the side of the bottle. Use a paper clip and wires to complete the switch.
6. Tape the two batteries together and tape one of the wires from the switch to the base of the batteries.
7. Join the wire from the other side of the switch to the bulb holder.
8. To complete the circuit, use a third wire to join the bulb holder to the top of the batteries.
9. Then stand the batteries inside the bottle or wedge them in with crumpled-up newspaper.
10. Glue or tape the funnel in position in the top of the bottle.

How it works
When you press down on the switch, you complete the circuit. Electricity flows from the batteries to the bulb, which lights up. The tin foil behind the bulb reflects the light back out of the torch so a wider beam of light shines out of the torch.

▶ A security worker uses a torch to check the lock on a gate.

Magic Magnets

More than 2000 years ago, the Ancient Greeks discovered a strange rock which could attract pieces of iron. Nearly 1000 years later, Chinese sailors used a piece of the same kind of rock to make a simple compass for their ships. If they hung the rock from a thread, they found that it always pointed North and South.

Nowadays, one name for this rock is **lodestone**, which means 'the stone that leads'. Another name is **magnetite**, which comes from the area of Magnesia, where the rock was first discovered. Materials with the same properties as magnetite can be made into magnets.

Looking at Magnets

Most modern magnets are made from iron or steel. Some are long and straight; they are called bar magnets. Others are shaped like a horseshoe. Small pieces of metal called **keepers** help to stop horseshoe magnets losing their magnetic force when they are not being used.

Magnetic Attraction

All you need is a magnet and a collection of things to test, such as a metal spoon, a glass jar, a plastic pot, keys, tin foil, coins, paper clips, an eraser, nuts and bolts, needles and pins, small stones and a pencil.

Try this experiment to see which materials are attracted to a magnet.

Touch the end of your magnet to each of the objects in your collection. Some of them will seem to stick to the end of the magnet as if they are glued there. Now try moving the magnet slowly towards each object and watch carefully. Small things will seem to leap towards the magnet. Put all the things that stick to the magnet in a separate pile. What are they made from?

More things to try

Does a magnet attract objects along its whole length or just at the ends?

How Strong are Magnets?

If you have several magnets, this experiment will help you to discover which one is the strongest.

Dip the end of one magnet into a box of dressmaker's pins or metal paper clips and, very gently, lift up the magnet. Lots of the pins or paper clips will cling to the magnet. Carefully pull them off and count how many you have picked up.

Now repeat the test with each of the other magnets in turn. Keep a note of the number of pins or paper clips each magnet attracts. The strongest magnet will pick up the highest number of pins or paper clips.

More things to try
- Can you find the strongest part of each magnet?
- Do both ends of a bar magnet have the same magnetic pull?
- Do bigger magnets have a stronger magnetic force than smaller magnets?
- Can you pick up more pins with both ends of a horseshoe magnet or with one end of a bar magnet?

▶ A magnetic catch helps to keep the door of a refrigerator shut. This is a safety device in case a small child climbs inside and shuts the door. If the door had an ordinary catch, the child would not be able to open it from the inside. But with a magnetic catch, the door can be pushed open from the inside.

There are also magnets inside other machines such as televisions, telephones and radios.

Warning
Do not put a magnet near a watch, a clock or a television screen. Magnets could damage these objects.

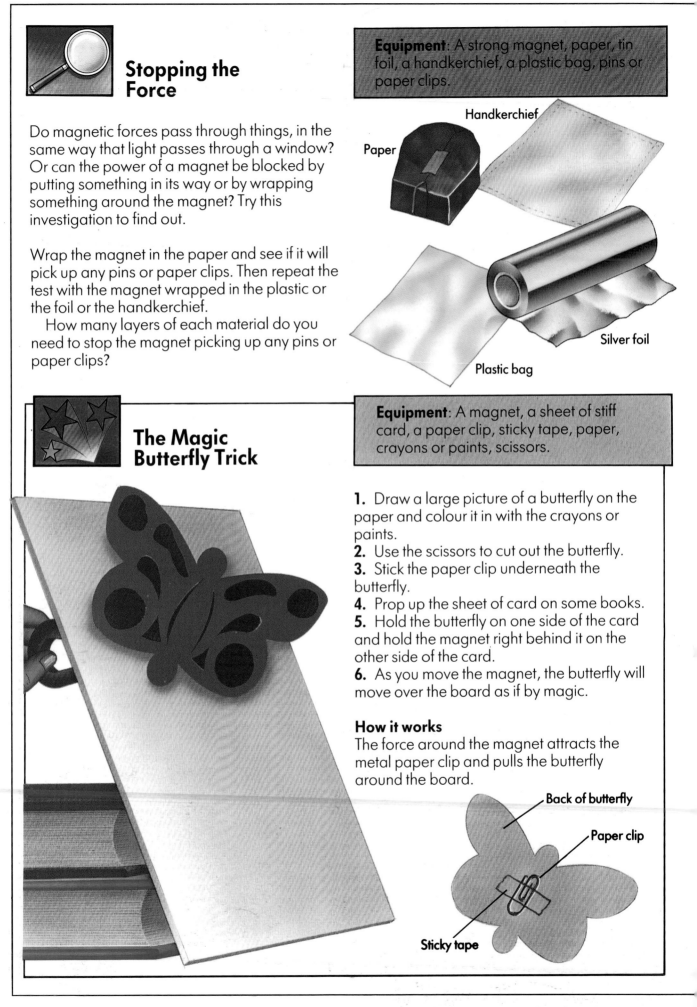

Stopping the Force

Do magnetic forces pass through things, in the same way that light passes through a window? Or can the power of a magnet be blocked by putting something in its way or by wrapping something around the magnet? Try this investigation to find out.

Wrap the magnet in the paper and see if it will pick up any pins or paper clips. Then repeat the test with the magnet wrapped in the plastic or the foil or the handkerchief.
     How many layers of each material do you need to stop the magnet picking up any pins or paper clips?

Equipment: A strong magnet, paper, tin foil, a handkerchief, a plastic bag, pins or paper clips.

Handkerchief

Paper

Silver foil

Plastic bag

The Magic Butterfly Trick

Equipment: A magnet, a sheet of stiff card, a paper clip, sticky tape, paper, crayons or paints, scissors.

1. Draw a large picture of a butterfly on the paper and colour it in with the crayons or paints.
2. Use the scissors to cut out the butterfly.
3. Stick the paper clip underneath the butterfly.
4. Prop up the sheet of card on some books.
5. Hold the butterfly on one side of the card and hold the magnet right behind it on the other side of the card.
6. As you move the magnet, the butterfly will move over the board as if by magic.

How it works
The force around the magnet attracts the metal paper clip and pulls the butterfly around the board.

Back of butterfly

Paper clip

Sticky tape

Make a Fishing Game

Equipment: A thin stick or garden cane, a large cardboard box, thin card, crayons or paints, paper clips, cotton or string, sticky tape, scissors, a small magnet.

1. Draw and colour ten fish shapes on the thin card and cut them out.
2. Write a different number on each fish.
3. Stick a paper clip on the back of each fish.
4. Decorate the large box to make it look like a fish tank and put the fishes inside the tank.
5. To make a fishing rod, tape or tie the small magnet to one end of some strong cotton or string. Tie the other end of the cotton or string to the stick or cane.

How to play the game
This game needs two players. Take it in turns to use the magnetic rod to pull a fish out of the box. To keep the score, count up the numbers on the fish you catch.

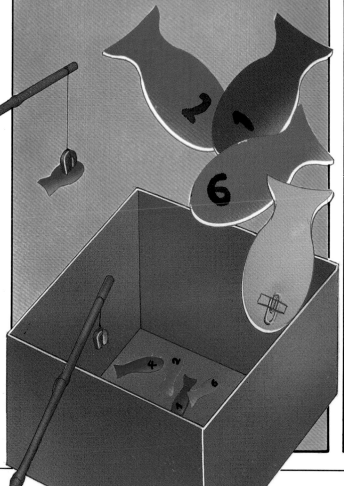

Magnetic Boating Game

Equipment: Magnetic fishing rods (see fishing game), pieces of cork, drawing pins, dressmaker's pins, paper, scissors, crayons or paints, sticky tape or glue, large bowl of water.

1. Make little boats from pieces of cork with a drawing pin pressed into the bottom. To make masts, stick steel pins into the corks.
2. For the sails, draw and colour paper triangles and cut them out. Glue or tape a sail to each mast.
3. Float the boats in the bowl of water.
4. Use the magnetic rods to steer the boats around the bowl and have boat races with your friends.

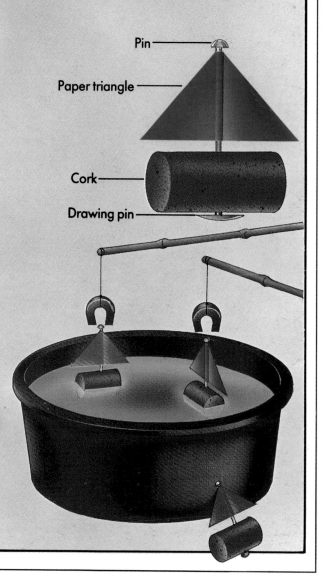

Pin

Paper triangle

Cork

Drawing pin

Test your Driving Skills

1. On the large piece of cardboard, draw and colour a system of roads. Make each road quite wide and include several road junctions, bends and a roundabout.
2. On the thin card, draw and colour a car as if you are looking at it from the side. Make sure the car is small enough to fit on to the roads you have drawn.
3. Cut out the top of the car but leave a flap of card at the bottom. Fold back the flap to make the car stand upright.
4. Push a drawing pin through the flap of card and put a piece of cork or modelling clay on top of the sharp point of the pin.

Equipment: A large piece of stiff cardboard about 30 to 40 cm (12 to 16 inches) square, thin card, crayons or colouring pens, scissors, drawing pins, modelling clay or cork, small magnet, a thin stick or cane, sticky tape, books or bricks.

5. Tape the magnet to the end of the stick or cane.
6. Rest the road system on books or bricks so it is high enough for you to be able to slide the magnet on its stick or cane underneath.

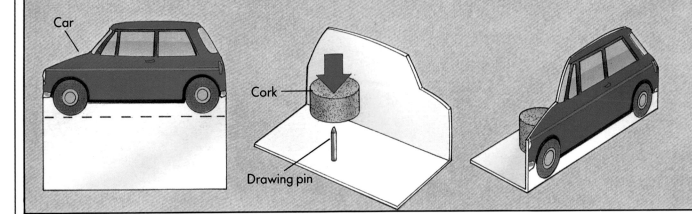

Car

Cork

Drawing pin

Paper Clip Trick

Put a large glass jar almost full of water on to a table. Drop a paper clip into the jar so it is resting on the side of the jar at the bottom. Can you get the paper clip out of the jar without getting your fingers wet?

If you hold a magnet outside the jar next to the paper clip and slowly slide the magnet up the side of the jar, it will pull the paper clip up with it. When you get to the top of the jar, the paper clip will stick to the magnet and you can lift it out of the jar.

How to play the game

This game needs one or more players. Start with the car in one corner and put the magnet underneath the cardboard directly below the cars. As you move the magnet, you will be able to drive the car along the roads. See how long it takes to drive the car around the course. Add a ten-second penalty every time the car comes off the road.

If your board is large enough and you have two magnets, you could have a race with a friend.

More things to try

With a large, flat board and two magnets on sticks, you can also make a magnetic soccer game. Make two goals from card, wood or wire and use a very light ball, such as a table tennis ball. The players can be made in the same way as the car. You will need to glue or tape strips of card around the board to stop the ball falling off the edge. See who can score the most goals.

Magnetic Forces

The strange invisible force that surrounds a magnet is not fully understood. But if iron filings are sprinkled on to a magnet they show the pattern of this force. The filings cluster together in places where the force is strongest. A lot of filings stick to the ends of the magnet. On the next three pages, you can find out more about these strong forces at the ends of a magnet.

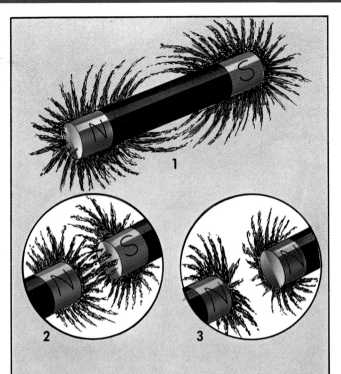

Iron filings show the lines of force around a magnet (**1**). Unlike poles attract each other (**2**); like poles repel each other (**3**).

Pushing and Pulling

The ends of a magnet are called **poles** and every magnet has a North Pole and a South Pole. The North Pole is sometimes red and the South Pole is sometimes blue or plain metal.

Tie a thread around a magnet so it balances horizontally when you let it swing freely. The magnet will turn so the North Pole faces North and the South Pole faces South. (You can check the direction with a compass.)

With two strong magnets, you can discover some fascinating facts about the poles of a magnet. Lay one magnet on a smooth surface and slide the other one towards it so a pole of one magnet is close to a pole of the other magnet. The two magnets will either spring together or try to push each other away. You will find that two North Poles or two South Poles will push away (repel) each other but a North Pole and a South Pole will attract each other.

More things to try

Tape a magnet on to the roof of a toy car and tape another magnet on to the roof of a second car. Make sure that the two North Poles or the two South Poles of the magnets are on the front of both cars. If you roll the two cars towards each other, the two like poles will repel each other and push the cars apart.

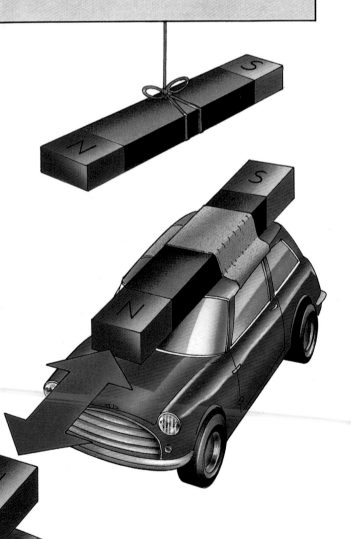

Magnetic Train

The force of strong magnets pushing away from each other is used in some high-speed trains. Both the train and the track contain powerful magnets which work only when electricity flows through them. This means they can be switched on and off.

The magnets are arranged so the North Poles of the track magnets face upwards and the North Poles of the train magnets face downwards. When the magnets are turned on, the two North Poles repel each other. This lifts the train clear of the track so it hovers above the rail. The train can move very easily like this and so it travels much faster than an ordinary train.

▲ The test run of the MLU-002 in Japan.

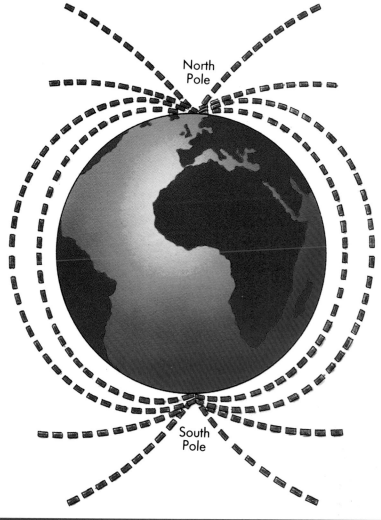

The Magnetic Earth

The Earth acts as if it has a gigantic bar magnet along its centre. Lines of magnetic force run through the Earth from one pole to another. The needle of a compass is a small magnet and it lines up with the Earth's magnetic field so it always points North and South. (The magnet in the experiment on page 30 pointed North and South for the same reason.)

A compass needle does not point to the true North Pole. Instead it points to a spot somewhere in Canada which is a long way to the west of the true North Pole. The Earth's magnetic forces are always changing slightly so the position of magnetic north changes slightly each year. Hundreds of years from now, magnetic north will be to the east of the North Pole. Magnetic south is also in a different place from the true South Pole.

Make a Compass

Equipment: A large needle, a small piece of cork or polystyrene, a magnet, a saucer of water.

First you need to turn the needle into a magnet; this is called **magnetizing** the needle. To do this, stroke one pole of the magnet gently along the whole length of the needle in the same direction 20 times.

Inside the needle, the little particles (**domains**) which make up the metal are usually pointing in different directions. As you stroke the needle with the magnet, the particles all line up and point in the same direction. As long as the particles stay in line, the needle will act like a magnet.

To make your compass, lay the magnetized needle on a piece of cork or polystyrene and float it in a saucer of water. The needle will swing round to point in a North-South direction, just like a real compass needle.

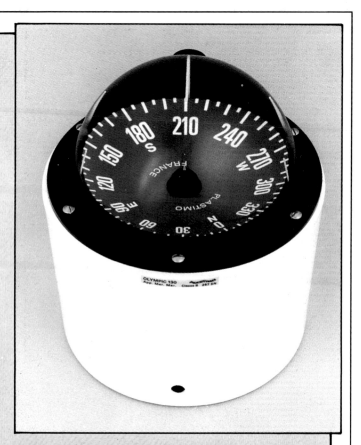

▲ A compass is especially important for navigating at sea. Nautical compasses are designed to stay level no matter how much the boat bobs up and down on the waves.

Domains pointing in different directions.

Domains lined up.

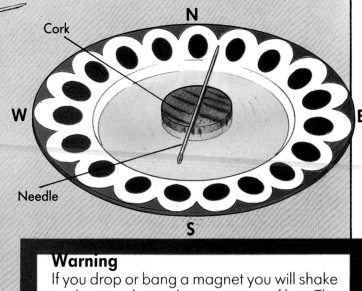

Cork

Needle

N

W

E

S

Warning
If you drop or bang a magnet you will shake up the particles so they move out of line. The magnet will then lose its magnetic powers.

Making Magnets with Electricity

In about 1820 a Danish scientist, Hans Christian Ørsted, discovered that electricity flowing through a wire close to a compass needle made the needle swing away from the North-South direction.

Scientists have since found many links between electricity and magnetism. For example, when electricity flows through a coil of wire which is wrapped around an iron or steel bar, the bar turns into a magnet. It is called an **electro-magnet**.

Make an Electro-magnet

Equipment: A battery, a switch (*see page 17*), an iron or steel nail about 15 cm (6 inches) long, some covered wire about 60 to 100 cm (2 to 3 feet) long, a box of pins or paper clips.

Battery

Switch

Nail

Electro-magnet

Pins

1. Join the wire to the battery and the switch.
2. Wind the wire around the nail about ten times.
3. Join the other end of the wire to the battery terminal to complete the circuit.
4. Switch on the electric current and dip the end of the nail into the box of pins or paper clips. What happens? Are any pins or clips attracted to your electro-magnet?
5. Switch off the current. What happens now?
6. Now wind the wire around the nail ten more times and repeat the experiment. Can you pick up any pins this time?
7. Finally, wind the wire in tight coils along most of the nail. (You may need to use some sticky tape to hold the wire in place.)
8. Repeat the experiment to see if the extra wire makes the magnet weaker or stronger.

How it works
The electricity flowing through the tight coils of wire creates a strong magnetic force from one end of the coil to the other. The force lines up all the magnetic particles in the nail and turns it into a magnet. With more wire coils, the magnetic force is stronger.

If your nail is made from iron, you will find that when you switch off the electricity, the pins or clips fall off the nail. Iron is only magnetic as long as electricity is flowing in the wire. It is a **temporary** magnet. But if your nail is made from steel, it stays magnetic even when the electricity is switched off. It is a **permanent** magnet.

Make an Electro-magnetic Crane

This crane will lift small steel objects when you switch on the electricity.

Equipment: An electro-magnet with an iron nail (*see page 33*), small cardboard boxes (two square ones and one long, thin one), a cardboard tube, two cotton reels, some strong thread, glue, sticky tape, scissors, paper clips or pins.

1. Make a hole in the top of both the square boxes.

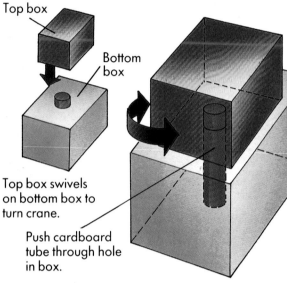

Top box

Bottom box

Top box swivels on bottom box to turn crane.

Push cardboard tube through hole in box.

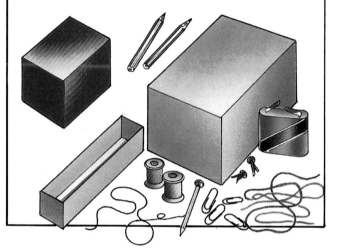

2. Push the cardboard tube down into one box and fit the other box on top of the tube.
3. Cut off both ends of the long, thin box.
4. Tie the thread to one cotton reel. Fix this reel in one end of the long, thin box by pushing a pencil through the side of the box and right through the middle of the reel.
5. Use another pencil to fix the other cotton reel in the other end of the long box and hang the thread over the top of the reel. Leave the thread hanging out of the box.

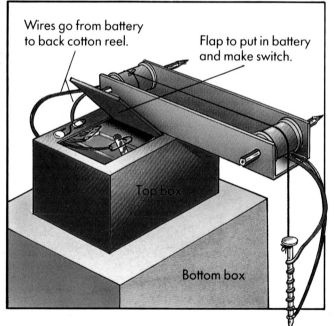

Wires go from battery to back cotton reel.

Flap to put in battery and make switch.

Top box

Bottom box

Pencil

Thread

Tie thread to back reel.

Hang thread over front reel.

Cotton reel

Tape pencil to reel to stop it turning round inside reel.

Stick long box to top of square box.

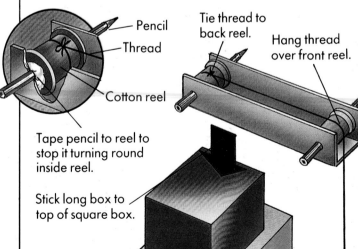

6. Glue or tape the long, thin box on top of the square box.
7. Put the battery inside the top square box and join it to a switch on the top of this box. Join the battery and the switch to the nail with some more wire, as shown in the diagram.
8. Lay the wires under the cotton reels and tie the nail to the end of the thread.
9. Decorate the outside of the crane with paints or crayons.

▶ Very large electro-magnets with iron cores are used to sort scrap metal. They attract all the iron and steel and separate them from the other metals.

10. Turn the crane so the nail is above the paper clips or pins. To lower the nail, turn the pencil on the back cotton reel.
11. To turn the nail into an electro-magnet, switch on the electricity. See how many pins are attracted to the nail.

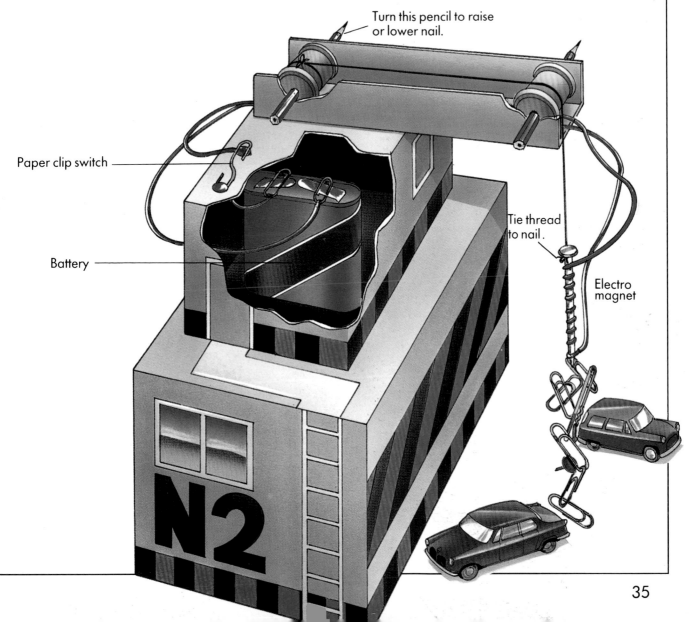

Turn this pencil to raise or lower nail.

Paper clip switch

Battery

Tie thread to nail.

Electro magnet

N2

Animals and Electricity

Most animals use electrical signals (**nerve impulses**) to send messages to different parts of the body. In humans, these messages travel through a network of nerve cells which link the organs of sight, hearing, smell, taste and touch to the brain. The brain is constantly sending and receiving electrical messages as it reacts to information about conditions inside and outside the body. The amount of electricity in our bodies is very, very tiny, but some animals, such as electric fishes, can generate massive amounts of electricity.

Electric Fishes

An electric eel (*above*) uses modified muscle cells along the sides of its body to generate electricity and respond to electrical signals. It can produce sudden, massive electric shocks of 500 volts, which could kill a horse or stun a person. It uses this electric power to capture and kill food or drive away attackers. Electric eels also produce low-voltage electrical signals which help them to find their way around and communicate with other fishes.

Passing on messages

At the point where one nerve cell meets another, there is a tiny gap called a **synapse**. When a nerve impulse reaches a synapse, it is changed from an electrical message into a chemical message. This can 'jump across' the gap and trigger an electrical nerve impulse in the next nerve cell.

Nerve impulses can travel at very high speeds. Some of the nerves inside our bodies can send impulses at 150 metres (490 feet) per second.

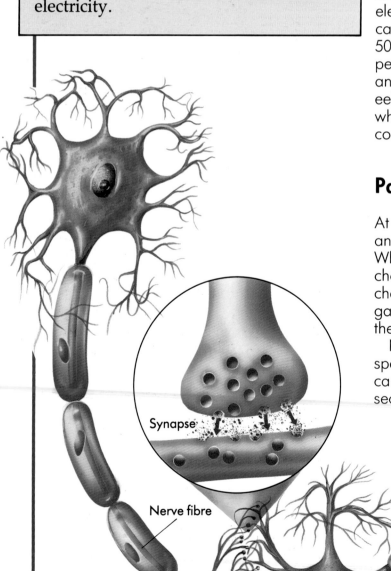

Synapse

Nerve fibre

Using Electricity

Electricity has changed our lives at home, at school and at work. Electric motors drive all sorts of machines, from vacuum cleaners to electric drills, which help us to do jobs more quickly and easily. We use electricity to keep warm in winter and cool in summer, and to provide light all the year round. Electricity works fans and air conditioning systems as well as refrigerators and freezers. Electricity makes pictures appear on television and computer screens. It can make clocks work and be used to switch machines on and off at set times. How do you think electricity might be used to help us in the future?

In the Hospital

In hospital, electricity powers X-ray machines, kidney machines (*see photograph below*), incubators for premature babies and all sorts of other vital equipment which helps people to recover from accidents or illnesses.

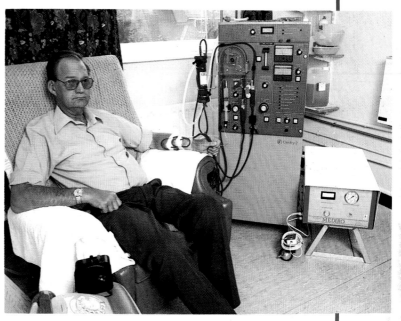

On the Farm

Farmers make use of many electrical machines, such as this milking machine. Machines help the farmer to give farm animals the right amount of feed. Young chicks can be reared under the warmth of electric heaters. Electric fans can be used to dry grain and keep it fresh, and electric conveyor belts make it easier to move straw and grain. Farming machines save time and do much of the heavy work.

In the Greenhouse

Automatic electric controls ensure that greenhouse crops are given ideal growing conditions all the year round, no matter what the weather is like outside. Electric thermostats control heating and ventilation and electric irrigation systems make sure the right amount of moisture reaches the plants.

Electricity for Transport

Electricity is a cheap form of power for some cars and trucks. These vehicles carry their electrical power in batteries which are large and very heavy; the batteries also have to be re-charged at frequent intervals when their electricity is used up. At the moment, there are no batteries which are small enough, light enough and powerful enough to make a car go fast for hundreds of miles. But one may be developed in the future. The advantages of electrically-powered vehicles are that they are quieter than vehicles with petrol or diesel engines and they do not pollute the atmosphere.

In the Factory

In factories, electrical machines such as fork-lift trucks (*above*) are used to move heavy objects from place to place. Tools such as electric drills, saws and paint sprayers also save a lot of time and heavy work.

Electricity drives the robots (*left*) which assemble products such as cars and computers faster and more accurately than people can. It also provides the heating for ovens and furnaces which melts metals or bakes clay into bricks.

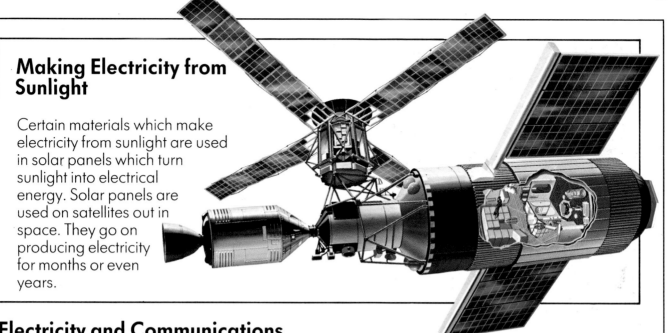

Making Electricity from Sunlight

Certain materials which make electricity from sunlight are used in solar panels which turn sunlight into electrical energy. Solar panels are used on satellites out in space. They go on producing electricity for months or even years.

Electricity and Communications

Electricity is vital for communication systems. Radios and television sets receive electro-magnetic signals transmitted from broadcasting stations. Telephones turn the sound of our voices into electrical signals which travel along the network of wires connecting telephones together.

The miniature electrical circuits in microchips have revolutionized the development of calculators and computers. A microchip contains thousands of electrical components on a piece of silicon smaller than a pin-head.

▲ In this picture of Chicago, you can see some of the street lights, car headlamps and light bulbs which light up the city at night. What would the picture look like if there was a power cut? Can you imagine living with only candles and fire to provide light, warmth and power?

◄ A wafer of silicon containing hundreds of microchips.

Index

Page numbers in *italics*
refer to illustrations, or to
illustrations and text
where these occur on the
same page

Editor: Nicola Barber
Designer: Ben White
Illustrators: Kuo Kang Chen
    Peter Bull
Consultant: Barbara Taylor

Cover Design: Terry Woodley
Picture Research: Elaine Willis

Photographic Acknowledgements
The publishers would like to thank the following for
kindly supplying photographs for this book:
Page 5 Ontario Science Centre, Toronto; 8 ZEFA;
9 ZEFA (bottom left), The Mansell Collection (top
right); 12 The Mansell Collection; 13 Launch Pad/
Science Museum, London; 16 Science Photo
Library; 22 Ann Ronan Picture Library; 23 ZEFA;
31 Science Photo Library; 32 PLASTIMO;
35 Science Photo Library; 36 I. Pulunin/NHPA;
37 Elga Ltd (top right), Holt Studios (bottom left);
38 Science Photo Library (top left), Austin Rover
(bottom left), Shell Photographic Library (right);
39 Plessey Semi-Conductors Ltd (left), ZEFA (right).

KINGFISHER
An imprint of Larousse plc
Elsley House, 24–30 Great Titchfield Street,
London W1P 7AD

This reformatted edition published by
Kingfisher 1997
10 9 8 7 6 5 4 3 2 1
Originally published by Kingfisher 1989
© Grisewood and Dempsey Ltd. 1989

A CIP catalogue record for this book
is available from the British Library.

ISBN 1 85697 372 7

Phototypeset by Tradespools Ltd., Frome, Somerset
Printed by South China Printing Company H.K.